BOO-COO DINKY DOW

Very Crazy in the Head in Vietnam (and Beyond)

DAN MATRISCIANI

ISBN: 978-1-53296-492-3

Interior and cover by The Book Couple

Printed in the United States of America

To our father and grandfather
on your seventieth birthday.
We know you believe "it don't mean a thing,"
but to us, this book means everything.

With all of our love, gratitude, and admiration.
We will never forget.

To Dan Hunt

ITS great being in
The group with you

Welcome Home
Dan

"We Ant right"

Contents

1

Hell's Jingle Bells

Thursday, December 24, 1964

Just another Christmas Eve riding in a delivery truck through the streets of Brooklyn. And me, just another eighteen-and-half-year-old being lugged around by one of his older (and bigger) brothers, Monty. Every soda truck driver has what is called a *helper*, which can be a misleading title, especially when the driver is your big brother, because as I was doing the heavy lifting, Monty was flirting with a girl on his soda route. It was our family business—not flirting (although Monty was good enough at it to have gotten the girl to marry him). Delivering beer and soda to the homes of people throughout New York City's second largest borough was what we Matriscianis did, even though liquid libation and sugary carbonation weren't always in the family. This was just the beginning of our family business.

In 1955, my father, Alex, sold Polly-O mozzarella door to door, which is how he met my mother, Adeline. He went to work for Municipal Haulage Trucking, because it was a better job—a job with a future. It seems she liked his cheese. My mother's father, Grandpa Montana referred to my father and his family as gypsies, because my grandfather, Daniel Matrisciani, was born in Egypt while his Napolitano parents traveled there to perform with a band of minstrels. When Daniel and his wife, Ada, came to America, Ada played piano and sang in an Italian opera theater on Canal Street at the Bowery in the East Village of Manhattan. The name was either the Amato Opera House or The Italian Opera House. Today, the theater is a Chinese bank. I have a recording of Ada singing with her oldest daughter, Elda, my aunt and my father's sister.

So, Alex, the son of music people, wound up on delivery trucks for Municipal until Municipal went out of business. In 1955, when my father found out he was out of a job, my mother, Adeline, who at the time was working in a sweat shop on 36th Street and 13th Avenue, sowing beads on women's sweaters, was pregnant with twins. I was the youngest of three boys already, and the twins would make the testosterone-filled brood five.

My mother's oldest brother, Uncle Nick, said he had some connections in the soda business and hooked up my father with a guy named, Sol, who owned a soda plant on 63rd Street and 15th Avenue in Brooklyn. He made a soda called Lord Cromwell, which had nothing to do with England. Nick lent my father some money to buy a soda route, and then my eldest brother, Alex Jr., whom everyone called Junior, bought a route, and Monty, the second oldest, bought a route from Paul, who married my mother's oldest sibling Uncle Nick's younger daughter, Jackie. And that's how I became Monty's helper on that Thursday evening.

Thursdays were always our late day, because we worked two routes in one. The early route was through the section of Brooklyn in which we lived and included Kensington, Bensonhurst, and Borough Park. The late route was in Clinton Hills around Myrtle Avenue, Bushwick, Fort Green, and Hall Street. Monty's future wife, Trudy, lived on Hall Street with her parents, Millie and Dom.

Do you know how long I had to sit in the truck waiting for Monty?

In between routes, when we left our section and headed for Clinton Hills, we'd pass our house to wash up, grab something to eat, and go to the bathroom. Running through the house, I was expecting to smell the beginnings of our traditional Italian seafood Christmas Eve feast, but instead, my mother and sister-in-law, Susan, were sitting at the kitchen table, crying.

"What's wrong?" I asked, thinking something must've happened to my brother Junior, who Susan was married to.

My mother didn't say anything, just handed me the envelope.

Greetings and Salutations
You are hereby ordered to report
to 39 Whitehall ST NYC
At 7 AM on January 4 Th 1965

Uncle Sam was resourceful enough to enclose in the envelope a fifteen-cent token to get me on the train downtown. I still have it. So I had a decision to make: get caught dodging the draft and live in an 8x12 prison cell or flee to Canada.

It took a few seconds to sink in, but once the reality hit me that I had been drafted, the last thing I wanted to do was hop back on that truck for the second route, although I didn't quite know what I would've done with the nervous energy that flooded through me. I felt restless, but didn't want to move. I felt like screaming but couldn't open my mouth. So, I did what Monty told me, figuring I better start practicing to follow orders, and got back on the truck.

We really only celebrated Christmas Eve in our house, because the adults in the family had nothing left after that. They partied so hard and stuffed themselves with squid, mussels, scungilli, sardines, and calamari (pronounced gah-la-mahd by the Italian Americans in our family) until it was time for them to head down to the basement to play cards into the wee hours. And of course, us kids always waited for Old Saint Nick to come, and he always coincidentally looked like Uncle Nick, as well as having the same name.

Before I was bitten by my draft notice booby trap, I had hoped that I'd be walking into a house filled with colossal chaos, because as long as someone was yelling at someone, everything was normal. Normal. That was me. Pretty normal. Naïve and sheltered, a young brother who looked up to his older ones. When Michael and Robert, the twins, came, I went from being the baby to smack in the middle. But still, I was as normal as anyone could expect to be. But, there was nothing normal about this Christmas. Nobody was arguing, the air in the house was static, nobody moved through the rooms with the thunderous vibrations of the subways that would take me downtown to White-hall Street in less than ten days.

2

A New Year's Eve Blackout

December 31, 1964

"So. You're going," Mr. Knight said to me, matter of fact, as if I had been called to jury duty.

"Have a drink," an expressionless Mr. Knight ordered, as he poured caramel-colored liquid into a rocks glass. I appreciated his gesture of pity, since I'd known him all my life. I imagined that for him, looking at me was like looking at his son, Ronny, who was one of my closest friends growing up. Ronny and I were heading to a New Year's Eve party, which I think was intended to keep my mind off of the fact that I might not see another New Year. Distracting me was an impossibility, but I didn't want Ronny to feel bad. I wasn't really a drinker, which is ironic now, but, man, was that one stiff drink. So stiff, I never made it out that night. Ronny took me home and drove himself to the party in my 1962 Oldsmobile Starfire.

I must have slept it off over the course of a few days, because the next thing I knew, it was January 2, and my mother was on the phone with a stranger. I knew it was a stranger for several reasons. One, she had her game face on, like she was about to yell at the milkman for being late. Two, she wasn't smoking. She needed all the oxygen to be able to speak in one long sentence to the man on the other line. "I'm calling to inform you that it is impossible for my son to report to Whitehall Street because the MTA is on strike and there is no way for him to get there so we are sorry but there's just nothing we can do about it."

Breathe, ma.

"Lady, give us your address, we'll send a car for him."

My mother wasn't the only one trying to find ways out for me, even though I never asked anyone to do so. One of mother's brothers (she had three, two older ones) Uncle Joe, who lived upstairs, told me he knew a local politician who could get me a six-month delay.

"Forget it," I told him. "Let's just get this over with."

3

Induction

January 4, 1965 · 6AM

I was driven by my father and mother to 39 Whitehall Street, said goodbye to the civilian world, and walked in to be officially inducted into the army. I looked at my mother and, as if I were five, my stare asked her, "Are you really going to leave me here?"

A guy in uniform led me into the induction room, which was quiet. I had never seen so many boys, hundreds of them, so pensive and still. Everyone looked unrested, but no one dared to lean their bodies against the ash-colored walls of the hall. Each one of us was inside our own heads, until the sergeant barked the first names on the list: "Adams, Timothy."

"Here," a voice cracked.

"Avery, John."

"Here," another voice coughed in the hall.

And on and on. My mind was reeling. I rewound to memories of my friend Ronald, whose name would be called shortly. I was the only one who knew he wasn't there to respond "here." And it wasn't because he was a draft dodger, which the army would be left to assume. He was a junkie who overdosed on his roof across the street from my house the week before. *He's probably better off.*

I have to admit, I was flat-out scared. I was one of the first among my friends to be drafted. It was still early in the war and I only knew what I knew from the fifteen minutes of news I watched a night, and that didn't tell us much at all. I knew every man would be taken; it was just a matter of when. Some of the guys were in collage. Some joined the Air Force or the Navy to avoid the army draft. And here I was with zero knowledge of what I was in for except for the important advice my Uncle Danny, my father's youngest sibling, and my Uncle Joe, my mother's younger brother, gave to me regarding army life. They told me, "The first and most important thing to know is NEVER RAISE YOUR HAND. NEVER VOLUNTEER."

I was remembering how serious their faces were but was snapped back into the hall by the roll call names. They were now at L. Making sure not to be seen or heard, I didn't stand too close to the front or the back. Then my name was called, so it was official: they had really meant to draft *me.*

To make matters worse the Marines had not filled their quota for the month and said they were looking for some of us in the room to volunteer. No one did. So, every fifth name that was called off the roster would become property of the Marines. When it came time for the letter M, I lost my breath and then found it again with a death rattle after my name wasn't called. It was the only time I would be grateful to be in the army.

After roll call, we were inducted into the United States Army by repeating the following:

I, Daniel Matrisciani, do solemnly swear that I will support and defend the Constitution of the United States against all enemies, foreign and domestic; that I will bear true faith and allegiance to the same; and that I will obey the orders of the President of the United States and the orders of the officers appointed over me, according to regulations and the Uniform Code of Military Justice. So help me God."

Led like cattle, our clumsy bodies stumbled on to green busses that took us from Whitehall Street to Grand Central Station, where we continued to be herded on to a train destined for Fort Jackson, South Carolina. It was the first time I was on a train that you could sleep on and use a toilet, and it was definitely the first time I had headed in the direction of south.

The train stopped, and my body shuddered awake at the shrill clanking of the steel. The doors opened, and in walked a uniformed man, yelling, "Get out, you no good pieces of shit, get the eff out now. Your Mama ain't here. You can't hide behind her skirt."

What. The. Hell.

"Line up. Get in line. I never saw such a sorry look-ing bunch of assholes!"

Then the words that smacked me upside the head harder than my father ever had.

"You'll all be dead the first day in Vietnam."

What? Who said anything about going to Vietnam? I'm not even assigned a squad or a billet yet. I was familiar with a billet, which is building you sleep in, because I watched a lot of old War War II movies.

"Move it, you hippie long-haired fags."

The first place I saw in South Carolina was the bar-ber's chair for the fastest haircut ever. I went in one door and came out another in sixty seconds flat. I felt like a sheep being sheared and looked as sheepish afterward.

The uniforms didn't fit any of us, and there was nothing that could be done about it while in basic training. In Ft. Jackson, I slept in a building that looks like a big gym, filled with cots and nothing else. The cots were close but not close enough to touch. When we were assigned to our permanent barracks we each had a six-foot space, which fit a bed, foot locker, and a wall locker. Your clothes had to be placed in a special way or you would get kitchen patrol and any other dirty duty the army could think of. It wasn't so bad considering that after the twins were born I had to sleep on a Castro convertible with my brother Monty. If I could do that, I could do anything. A day and a night of that was the beginning of my breaking in, the way they do horses—cracking whips, whistling, and yipping.

"Line up you dumb asses. Get in line. Follow me. Spread out. One grenade will kill you all."

WHAT?

"Sit on the ground," the sergeant ordered sadistically.

There were hundreds of "men," all of us, sitting when being told to stand, standing when being told to sit. Fumbling fools completely turned upside down (even when we should have been right side up).

The first night in our permanent barracks, the drill sergeant asked thirty or so of us, "Who here knows how to dance?" The biggest dummy raised his hand and had a mop and bucket thrown at him and was ordered to mop the floor.

Never volunteer.

This was orientation in to the army. It was a nightmare. We were told things like:

"If you have someone to write to you better do it. And don't exaggerate your situation. If the commander gets a phone call from one of your mamas, he ain't gonna like it, and if he don't like it, the captain won't like it, and if he don't like it, the lieutenant won't like it, and if he don't like it, *I* won't like it.

DO YOU ASSHOLES NOW UNDERSTAND THE CHAIN OF COMMAND?

Yes, sir!

If we did receive letters from friends and family while in Vietnam, we had to burn them after reading them, so I have none of the correspondence now. It really was not a nice thing to make us do.

We were finally assigned a platoon number and barracks. They were built for WW1 and still looked brand new because you could not walk down the center of the room. The barracks which were just long two-story wood-frame buildings with a basement that had a coal-burning furnace. Each night someone had to stand fire watch. Not to look out for fire but to keep the fire going. If you let the fire go out, the barracks would get cold, and the guys would get cold. The next night, as punishment for letting the place get cold, you received a GI shower. The person responsible for the fire going out would be taken out of bed while sleeping and dragged into the shower and beaten with a bar of soap in a sock. This also was done if your hygiene was not up to par. Or anything else that affected the people in the barracks as a whole.

For the next three days we'd be taking aptitude tests that would determine what we'd do in the army. "Take them seriously."

As if anything around here could be mistaken for a joke.

When we weren't taking tests, we were running and

doing calisthenics. I knew I was going to get in shape. But until I started basic I had no idea what calisthenics were *really* like. This was not high school PE. In basic, run, dodge, and jump was the most consistent form of exercise training. It's just what it sounds like except you add a mile-and-a-half run in under seven minutes with boots on.

Running, we were always doing double time; never walking, always running. We would do ten-mile marches and run some and double-time some. We would do jumping jacks and drop right into squat thrusts, right into pushups to standing position and then start all over again. There was a hill we called suicide hill, because after a long day of physical strain, the drill sergeant would end with having us run up that hill. Guys would throw up. The drill sergeants would yell all day long, "Listen to me; I'm trying to save your life." The conditioning worked. It took some time, but it all got much easier.

At the end of basic you had to pass the physical test. If you failed the test you would get recycled and have to do basic all over again with a new group. The test consisted of climbing over walls, crawling under barbed wire, running with live machine gun fire over your head. You had to low crawl on your stomach, so low that when we low crawled to the mess hall, which we did every day for every meal, we were told to take our shirts off and put them on backwards and have the guy behind you button them so you wouldn't tear the buttons off. All that low-crawl training comes in handy while live ammo is whipping over your head. That phrase, "How low can you go" isn't from a song, it's from the low crawl.

Because I was hunting with my Uncle Mike and my two older brothers since I was sixteen, I was looking forward to the rifle training. The first question asked by the sergeant in charge of the rifle training was, "Anyone ever shoot a rifle before?" Being from Brooklyn and remembering what my uncles had told me, I did not raise my hand, even though I had been shooting since I was fourteen. The sergeant tells one of the dopes that put his hand up to come over to him. He then tells the class that we should not be afraid of the recoil from the rifle. Then he shoots at the target 100 yards away and doesn't flinch over the kickback.

Turning to look at the volunteer, the sergeant says, "You won't feel a thing." He proceeds to place the butt of the rifle against his groin and shoots at the target again.

"Tell the class if *that* hurt," the sergeant said to the volunteer as he crouched to the floor, white as a ghost. I never heard the answer because we were laughing so hard. And *we* were going to save the world from Communism?

Apparently I had some mechanical skills, and would be receiving my Advanced Individual Training (AIT) in helicopter maintenance and become an E4, the same rank as a corporal, but a specialist. I didn't know a thing about helicopters, but I was sort of excited. I would be going to Ft. Rucker in Dothan, Alabama, to go to the U.S. Army Aviation School. I can still hear my platoon sergeant, Sergeant Baskett, when I read my orders after graduation from basic that were posted on the bulletin board, and I said I was not going to the infantry. My AIT would be in aviation instead of becoming a ground soldier.

"So, you're happy?" Baskett asked with a snarl.

I was more surprised that I tested that well, and actually learned something about myself.

A mechanic. Not bad.

"I wouldn't be so happy. Where do you think all the Hueys are going?" he asked, pointing to a black-and-white glossy photo of a helicopter taped to the wall.

"Vietnam, Sir."

4

Private First Class Matrisciani

After aviation school, I finally felt like a person again. No one was calling me a fag or a mama's boy or an asshole. The first thing I had to do was see the tailor to get my assembly line fatigues looking sharp and custom fit. The man was nothing like the small Italian tailors we had in Brooklyn, who yelled at you in broken English to turn around and didn't care if they pricked you with their pins as they marked the spot with white chalk for the hem. Not that I needed a tailor back home, since my mother was our in-house seamstress. This tailor was tall and thin, and took his job seriously. He put elastic in the bottom of my pants legs so I could blouse them over the top of my boots. And it's incredible how far creases in the pant leg can go to make you feel dressed up. It was like the Emperor's New Clothes, all smoke and mirrors—take the Brooklyn boy and instantly make him look

17

distinguished, like he belonged on a helicopter instead of underneath it.

School is a blur. There was a lot a classroom instruction and hands-on with helicopters. What isn't a blur is that we were allowed weekend passes. Another horse-breaking maneuver—the handfed carrot after I'd been broken. Finally I had graduated from subhuman to somewhat-human. I hadn't had a weekend of freedom since I left Brooklyn, or more accurately, before I read my draft notice.

The company was filled with a good number of guys from places like North and South Carolina, Louisiana, Arkansas, and so on. You could tell by the way they talked, but mostly by their reaction to the way *I* talked! And all of them unanimously agreed that it was not a good idea for me, or my pal, Joe, from South Philly, to head out into Dothan. "Y'all are Yankees." But they were more worried about Joe because he was black, although my being an Italian Catholic from New York was a close second to lynch mob bait. Joe had the good sense and the unfortunate first-hand experience to agree that going out was a bad idea.

So we went.

I didn't start throwing the term "I reckon" around or anything, but I did have my first taste of moonshine. There were about eight of us that night, passing the jug around, and it turned out Joe was the fastest runner. But not before we got some good shots in. Lesson learned. The scent of Yankee blood leaves a trail. (I'd take that wisdom back with me to Dothan after I get back from Nam.)

May

I had my orders to report to Vietnam, but not until I returned from a two-week leave that would allow me to go home to celebrate my nineteenth birthday. My father could not understand how a grown man like me could not do any kind of work for two weeks, so he put me to work. Truthfully, all of my friends were drafted or enlisted and the only guys left were the dopers and 4F people, and I wanted nothing to do with them. So I worked as a helper on the trucks and was passed around between three drivers like a hot potato. My birthday, May 4, was spent on the truck.

I left for Nam with little fanfare. My father and mother drove me to Idlewild Airport, now the famous JFK International Airport, along with my twin ten-year-old brothers in the back of my father's Lincoln. My first stop was San Francisco. When I got to the gate, the airline attendant told me that my ticket indicated I was at the wrong airport. My mother unleashed on my father, as if it were his fault. I felt so bad for him that I wanted to take off my green dress uniform and give it to him so he could get on the plane just to escape her wrath. We needed to get to LaGuardia

Airport in northern Queens ASAP. My father jumped on the Grand Central, all the while my mother asking him what the hell was wrong him, and how he could be so stupid. We got there in the nick of time. I was so immature I couldn't get myself to the right airport. Nam was going to be interesting . . .

The plane to San Francisco was a packed commercial airliner. I sat next to a guy named Bob, who I was in basic with. We noticed the most peculiar thing. When we landed in San Francisco, more soldiers got on the plane and fewer civilians boarded. We weren't allowed off at these layovers, by the way. When we landed in Hawaii, again more solders and fewer civilians boarded, and by the time we landed in Guam, the only civilians on the plane were the flight attendants, which back then we called stewardesses.

There was no layover in San Francisco, only a twenty-minute layover in Hawaii. Finally, we were allowed to get off the plane, and Bob and I headed to the airport bar and ordered a drink called a Zombie. The glass was tall and shapely, as if I were drinking on the beach, and sadly, I didn't have enough time to finish it before we had to board. We did, however, have a three-hour layover in Guam. I know the army somehow got that done on purpose, since we all were quite aware it was our last stop before Vietnam.

Overall, it took us more than twenty hours from New York to Vietnam, and I was numb for most of it, completely shut down so I wouldn't have to deal with rambling thoughts about what was about to happen. When the plane started its final approach, anyone who was talking, stopped. It was as quiet as a church, and it was the first time I allowed my thoughts to come through. We were all in our own heads now. *What were the people going to be like? How hot is it? Are all the stories the sergeants told us going to be true?* The world was large back then, and I didn't know if the people were going to be in grass skirts or naked, like tribal people. What I found was a civilization that was over 1,000 years old. What I did not know is that they were at war with someone for most of that time. We were going to be another pimple on their ass.

5

FNGs in the Iron Triangle

Saigon, Command Base, May 1966

We landed in Tan Son Nhat Airport in southeastern Vietnam after flying for a full day. Tan Son Nhat was not only an airport but an army base—a huge one—so we didn't have to leave the airport on arrival. Most of the GIs already there were shirtless because it was so hot, but we were told to stay in uniform, or else we FNGs (fucking new guys) might get lost in the crowd of bare flesh. The buses that would transport us the next day had wire mesh over the windows, and looked like cages, which immediately brought a question to mind about why a bus would need mesh. The question was answered by the bus driver, an army corporal, who told us the mesh would prevent us from catching the grenades that the Vietcong (VC) threw. *Great.*

Talking to solders while we were milling around I was told not to underestimate the VC, who would stoop to anything to win their civil war. They wanted the foreigners out the country, to be united, and go back to growing rice. The VC were going to fight hard, just like they when they defeated the French and the Japanese and the Chinese.

The bus stopped in front of a large Quonset hut— a prefab steel structure that doubled as headquarters for army ops. I got off the bus with everyone else to be assigned to our units.

"Does anyone know how to type?" asked a sergeant.

To my surprise Bob said, "I do."

"Okay, you are now the company clerk."

I had only started to take typing lessons while I worked for RCA Communications after high school graduation, and I told Bob I was jealous that he could type.

"I *can't* type," Bob confided. "But it sure beats humping the bush. You should have said something."

"I don't like to tempt fate," I replied.

A few months later on a flight to Saigon I went looking for Bob, and was told he was killed in a mortar attack. Forty years later, when I finally had the nerve to visit the wall at the Vietnam Memorial in Washington, D.C., I didn't look for Bob's name because I prefer to think the guy who told me Bob was killed was just being an ass.

6

The Robin Hoods

We were in the Mai Cong Delta in a 120-square mile area in the Binh Duong Province known as the Iron Triangle, which was named for the stronghold of the Viet Minh activity during the war. The region was under the control of the Viet Nimh during the French War. The main base camp of the infantry–known as the Big Red One—was adjacent to our base camp. From the air, you knew exactly where the Big Red One lived, because the infantry cleared the jungle in the form of a number 1. In order to have a base camp, the infantry needed to clear the three-tier canopy jungle— a jungle that makes it impossible to see the sky—so an attack on the base would not be easy. To do so, the army forested by spraying weed killer on the jungle. Well, in a week the jungle was gone. The spray was called Agent Orange.

I was now a helicopter mechanic assigned to a unit known as The Robin Hoods. The Robin Hoods consisted of slicks and gunships, both are helicopters, with slicks being used to carry troops, and gunships used to attack from the air. I lived in a tent in the maintenance area, where I would do major mechanical work—replacing skids, doors, rotor blades, and doing electrical work—on all helicopters (ships). When the crew chiefs responsible for small maintenance on their ship couldn't make the repairs, they'd "Red X" the ship and hand it off to me and the other mechanics for surgery.

I took my first helicopter flight when I was taken from Saigon to Lai Khe where I was going to spend the next year of my life. It was like being in a race car. We flew at about 1500 feet with the doors open. All I saw was trees, but preferred to look straight ahead, staring into the sky as the horizon drew me in. We traveled thirty-five miles north to Lai Khe, a rubber tree plantation that belonged to the French. I was ordered not to damage any of the trees while doing maintenance on the troubled Hueys.

What about the VC mortars? Do they count as a reason to shoot a moving tree?

There, I met some of the guys who had already been living there. With me joining the crew, there were eight of us mechanics. I was a replacement for someone who rotated home. I was shown around the compound—the mess hall, the shower, which consisted of ply wood and half a screen. The toilets were enclosed the same way. I used the word *toilet* loosely—certainly the French would be insulted to use their language to describe the facilities. Basically, picture a bench with a hole in it with a fifty-five-gallon drum cut in half beneath it.

That should cut the reading time down in the john.

It would rain so hard that the entire area would've flooded unless we built a drainage system to send the water back into the jungle. Slits in the earth acted like our own pipeline—a series of trenches, three feet wide and two feet deep.

So I went to work. I was assigned to the main maintenance building. We fixed the ships the crew chiefs could not. We pulled out engines and changed transmissions. It was okay work, but I kept looking at the sky full of ships, knowing I had to be a crew chief. I had my reasons. The first being I was nineteen years old and stupid. The second reason was getting paid $55.00 more a month. The third reason was that we were getting mortared almost every night, and I didn't like going into the bunkers, because we built them ourselves and that scared me even more. If that drill sergeant in South Carolina was right when he told us on the train that I was going to die in Vietnam, I wanted a fighting chance, and that chance was in the sky. I wanted to be on the ship, in charge of its maintenance as crew chief, so when our camp was mortared, I'd receive orders to take off after the VC who had just attacked us. Becoming a crew chief would allow me to play two roles – maintenance man would be my alter-ego when I became gunner.

The ships had crossbows with quad-60 machine guns and two rocket pods. That was the way to go. Add

26

to that, two M60s at each door, operated by the crew chief (first gunner) and second gunner. Later on, the army used mini guns (modern Gatling guns). WOW! What fire power. So I spoke to the sergeant in charge of the crew chiefs and told him I wanted to be assigned as a crew chief but only to the crossbows, which were the helicopters with the guns on them. I didn't want to be on a slick because they were mainly troop carriers, and that wouldn't do me any good after a mortar attack. The sergeant promised that the first opening would be mine. But not so fast. It wasn't that easy. He told me this reassignment meant I would have to change my MOS (Military Occupational Specialty) from 67n10 to 67n20 (helicopter mechanic) and then qualify for my combat wings. Unfortunately to do that I only had two weeks, since one of the gunships was hit, wounding the crew chief. They needed a replacement pronto.

7

Meeting TZ

Aside from the fact that explosives were fired at our company area and we would go into the bunkers almost every night, there was another reason I didn't like going into the bunkers. As I said before we built them. One day (I guess it was a slow war day) just right before I was assigned crew chief to my own ship, 419, which I named "Nickel and Dime 4-1-9" because it rhymed, I was ordered to help fill sand bags with three guys who were already hard at work. Sand bag detail was real fun in the hot sun. The sand was trucked in from the beautiful beaches of Vietnam and we used our entrenchment tool, which was a small shovel, and filled the potato-sack-sized bags until they weighed about forty to fifty pounds, and placed them in a semicircle around the front of the helicopter to protect it from scrap metal from the motors. We also built a bunker over a hole in the ground so we could go inside during a mortar attack. As I joined the group, I overheard two guys from California ranking out this skinny kid.

"I'm Dan from Brooklyn," I said, interrupting the joking.

"Oh, great," one of the surfers said to the other, "another guinea from New York."

Excitedly, the skinny kid spoke over the riotous laughter. "Hi! I'm TZ from Gunhill Road in the Bronx."

The Bronx? He might as well be from Mars.

Until being drafted, I had never been out of Brooklyn, and the most I knew about the Bronx was that the Yankees played there, and I was more a football fan than anything. But it didn't matter that I knew nothing about his borough and him mine; we were two Italians from New York City, and we instinctively knew that if we stuck together nobody could be a match for us. To this day, Tony (TZ) and I are still a tag team. Not a day goes by that we don't talk on the phone. He calls me "brother," and I, him. My grown kids and their children call him "uncle," and our friendship is sacrosanct. It's one of the many things I brought back with me from Vietnam, except I wouldn't ever change this one.

Still breaking our backs working on sand bag detail, one of the guys from California, who thought I was a pretty good sport, introduced himself as Ron. It turns out that when I got assigned as crew chief to the Nickel and Dime 4-1-9, Ron was my gunner. We flew every day together. I still speak to Ron all the time, even though he went back to California after Nam. Everyone in the company knew how tight the three of us were, but there was actually a fourth in our posse,

Ron L, also a chew chief. He rotated home earlier because he was there first. Now, he's a card dealer in Vegas, and we're still in touch.

To make the transition from mechanic to crew chief, I had to go through a brief training period in which Tony, who was a crew chief, volunteered to train me. Becoming a crew chief meant that the only ship that I would be responsible to do maintenance work on was the Nickel and Dime, whereas when I was a mechanic, I was assigned to whatever helicopters needed work. Becoming a crew chief also meant that when I wasn't on the ground fiddling around with tools, I was in the air, shooting a 30-calibre M60 machine gun with a second gunner, a pilot, and a copilot.

On the first day of training, the helicopter took Tony and me up. I took one side of the ship, shooting out of an open doorway, and he took the other side. My exercise was to be able to shoot at and hit a barrel from about 800 feet. But the helicopter wasn't still, and each time I found the barrel, the pilot would purposely turn the ship, and I'd lose sight of it over and over again. Ultimately, the swirling ship dizzied me and the moving target below made my eyes cross. Tony couldn't stop laughing at the sight of my frustration. I wanted to earn my combat wings, and I'd have to get through this field training with flying colors if that was going to happen.

By the time I became acclimated, I realized that I

needed to shoot from the left side of the ship at all times because from the right side you had to shoot upside down, and I didn't like the idea of that. From the right side, you have to mount the machine gun on a bungee cord upside down because the empty brass (shells) eject out of the right side of the gun. When you shot the gun, the brass would eject outside the door and if they hit the tail rotor, we'd crash. So, to combat that, we hung the gun upside down so the brass could eject *into* the ship. The left side didn't pose these complications, so once I was out of training, Ron took the right side and shot upside down, which is a bit apropos considering Ron's upside down behavior half the time.

On one of my first combat training flights with Tony I had my first taste of trouble. Now, this was not a mock flight. I was training, but we were really going in. Tony was the crew chief of his own ship, the 1-8-9, and that's where I trained. The crew on Tony's ship that day consisted of a pilot, copilot, a gunner (me), and crew chief (Tony). When our ship was on standby, we basically waited for a siren to sound off, similar to a fire engine's, jumped out of our tents, and ran out to the flight line. As crew chief, Tony's job was to untie the rotor blade before the pilot and copilot arrived. My job for that day, and the job of every gunner, was to uncover the mini guns and rocket pods. The pilot started the ship and we were off to the Mai Cong Delta to help out the Big Red One, which was taking heavy ground fire.

At the risk of sounding too romantic, I do have to admit that as the sun came up, the beauty of the land below made the whole situation feel surreal. A few months ago, I was loading soda on to a truck, and here I am earning my wings. Not bad for a guy from Brooklyn with just a high school diploma. And then out of my peripheral, I caught a glimpse of the left side of the ship, and as much as I hoped it was the sun's glare playing tricks on me, I knew I had royally screwed up.

"Oh shit," was all I could utter into my helmet mic, which was hooked to Tony's helmet.

"What?"

I motioned with my hand to the door next to where I was sitting, as if my words through the mic weren't clear enough, and said, "Look out my door."

"You shittin' me? You didn't take the gun covers off?" Tony's usual laid back nature was replaced by an immediacy and annoyance I hadn't witnessed from him before. "If they get blown off, they will wrap around the tail rotor. And we're dead men."

This was going to be such a stupid way to die, I thought. I could hear the mourners at my wake whispering behind my distraught mother's back at her family's Brooklyn funeral parlor: *That Danny, he wasn't really able to do much more than work on that soda truck. Never even got to earn his wings in Nam.*

Tony's bellow snapped me back into reality. "Climb out on the skids and get them."

"Are you nuts? I'm not going out there."

The only other option I had was to tell the pilots we had to land, and that was as much a suicidal option, maybe even more. *I should just climb out on the skids and jump off. It'll be an easier and faster way to die.* Tony broke the news to the pilot for me, and without a word, the pilot found a small clearing in the Delta. We came in hard and fast. The infantry was taking a beating and the longer we were on the ground, the more at risk we were, so we diverted two gun ships from helping the infantry to cover our ass while I took the gun covers off. It seemed like hours that we were on the ground, but it was more like ninety seconds.

Back in the air and still heading for the Mai Cong, I knew I had messed up big time, but I needed to deal with that later because we were about to go into battle. As we flew and shot tens of thousands of rounds and hundreds of rockets, we refueled and reloaded so many times, my whole body was sore, using muscles I didn't know you had. We flew back to our base at Lai Khe in the late afternoon just before dusk. We were out for at least twelve hours.

The most I stayed out was for three days, when we were on an operation mission. Because we were travelling farther, it would be a waste to fly back to home base to reload and refuel, so we'd do so at any base. We slept on the ship. Some guys drew a hammock up from one side of the width of the ship to the other. I just slept on the floor. The old "roll up your vest and sleep," which we didn't get much of and which we didn't need anyway. Sleep was for old people and babies. We thought we were neither.

When a dozen Huey gunships come in from the same company, it's quite a spectacle, and it was my favorite part of being out on long missions. Imagine you're marching as a unit in cadence. Everybody is in step with each other and coordinated ... left face, right face, about face. You've done a good job in battle. All of the helicopters are returning to base as air control says over the mic, "Welcome back, Robin Hoods, you were outstanding." In those moments I was a member of a proud organization—The Robin Hoods. War, after all, is a team sport. The ships would come in and hover over each landing pad, like hummingbirds over honeysuckle. On command and in simultaneous motion, each helicopter of the squadron, following the lead ship, made a right face and set down. Sometimes this choreography is enhanced with special effects—if you consider smoke cans filled with red, green, or yellow smoke special.

Smoke was used to determine how safe certain landing zones were. If one of us ships got shot at from the jungle, we'd drop a red can to mark the spot that the shooting was coming from to alert our slicks that were carrying up to five troops at a time, that they shouldn't land there. Sometimes it looked as if Jackson Pollack had come to save the day with brightly colored drips of primaries. Yellow indicated the landing zone was considered cautious—either we weren't sure, or were shot at from proximities nearby enough that we could assume the area was soon to be infested. I don't remember ever throwing green, which meant safe, because I only remember being shot at, even though I was on a gunship. And let me tell you, you have to be insane to fire at a gunship, because there's too much firepower being reciprocated from the air.

One day when coordinating our pomp and circumstance Robin Hoods landing, one of the gunners did not have a glove on to protect his hand from the hot can, and in pain dropped the can of smoke and burned down a village hut.

After our Hollywood landing, the pilot came to the flight line and reamed me out for what seemed to be hours. I think every officer was waiting to kick my ass for making the mistake with the gun covers. I don't know how many officers we had in the company but I do know we had forty-four majors, and considering I had to stand and be told that I was an ass by every single officer, it was pitch dark before they were through with me.

Later on in the night a young lieutenant tried to lift my spirits. "Don't let this get to you, he said. "You have the rest of the year to make up for this day."

I had only been in Vietnam eight weeks.

8

Getting What I Wished For

So now I am trained and have my own ship, the 4-1-9, and Tony and I planned to try to always try to be on the same missions. Gunships never flew in a combat situations alone. We were either in a light fire team (two ships) or a heavy fire team (three ships). When my ship made a gun run, we'd head for the ground, our door gunners opened up to protect our six, mini-guns and rockets blazing at the tree tops, then bank into a hard 180-degree turn away from the target, which is a vulnerable position for a ship to be in. Then the other ship would do the same thing so your ship had cover when pulling away from the target area.

There were all kinds of flight missions: search and destroy, battle operations, convoy cover, brown water boat cover, PT boats in the rivers and milk runs for supplies. Not really for milk, but food, discharge, and a bottle of scotch. The best was battle ops. Second best was search and destroy. Convoy cover and brown boat cover sucked.

With battle ops, you were in a fight that was coordinated from the ground and you got to hear the ground commander telling the gunships where to place their fire. On operation Manhattan, the electric system for the mini guns and rocket went out. While Ron was trying to fix it in the hell hole, I hooked up my M60 (560 rounds per minute) with the mini gun ammo so I wouldn't have to reload, while keeping the barrel of the 60 cool by keeping it as far out the door as I could without falling out. I heard through my helmet someone on the ground say, "Keep hitting the tree line! You just shot four VC off my back, then the pilot responds, "Same-same, mini gun." That was my command to keep doing whatever it was I was doing.

I was the only one shooting, and it's not the same as when more than one gun is going off. It was so quiet. We were a moving target because we were just flying straight over the tree line. I finally redeemed myself from the gun cover debacle. Ron got the guns up after about ten minutes, and we were back in the fight. You couldn't leave a fight because the men on the ground needed us.

Ron didn't always fly with me. We had our gunners assigned to us on a daily basis. One day we were flying over the Village of Bear Cat, and I had a new gunner. We were over a Buddhist temple and a monk came out waving his arms as to gesture go away. We were just flying over; the monk was on the right side of the ship, Smithy's side, when Smithy opened up on him with his 60. He just cut him in half.

"Why did you do that?" my voice squealed, giving away my terror.

"I don't know." He looked and sounded like a robot, his empty stare matching his lifeless words.

He didn't come back to the unit. I'm not sure what the army did with him.

One night my company was awoken and ordered to go to the tree line right before the runway. *What the F is going on? Why were we with our M14s hiding in the tree line; we are an aviation company, not infantry.* We were told that the Big Red One (infantry) was going to be attacked, and if the VC got through the tree lines, we would be next. Why aren't we in the air with our gunships? I remember being really scared and unequipped to handle this possible attack. I was used to combat from the air, not on the ground, although when speaking to the grunts (infantry) who humped the jungle, they would tell us *we* were nuts to be flying in a Huey. I guess it's whatever you get used to. Where I was taking cover under a rubber tree, this one aviation guy from my unit, put himself right in front of me. I scared the shit out of him when I said, "Good position. Too bad I will have to shoot *you* first." He moved fast. You could hear small arms (rifles and machine guns) fire in the distance for what seemed like forever. I never peed so much in my life, wondering if the VC were going to get through the Big Red One and infiltrate our tree line, where we were just sitting ducks. Finally the order came to stand down. The Big Red One had done its job and we could go back to tents. When we asked why we did not fly and use the gunships, we were told it would have been too close for our ground guys' safety. It hit me. We are in an effing war.

As I got accustomed to Vietnam and to life at the base in the village of Lai Khe, Tony, Ron, and I were almost always together. We would find a way to be in the same place at the same time. I even got Ron to become my full-time gunner? I went to the sergeant in charge of the crew chief and asked him to ask the sergeant in charge of the gunners to make it happen. So it did. The pilots wanted to fly with Tony and me because we got care packages from home with all the good Italian stuff. So instead of C-rations for lunch, we would have a feast.

The village was across the runway of our base camp. We would bribe the MPs (military police) to let us pass the wire, and we would bring the girls to our tents five at a time. This went on until the officers started to get jealous and ordered us to "stop doing that thing with the girls."

To go to the village you had to take you're M14 because the village was not secure. So, then why would you go there? We were twenty years old, and, well … you know. One guy would stand guard while the other went inside the hut. The French owned-company

Michelin Tires had a chateau at the end of the village, which once secured, became army headquarters. We'd go there and use the swimming pool with the girls. Some things were funny like the time I said to a pilot, "How about a barbeque tonight?"

"Okay," he answered. "Go shoot a water buffalo."

We flew six days a week, eight to twelve hours a day. Sometimes we would get only one hot meal a day and eat in the mess hall, which was open all night. No matter how late you came in, you could get something to eat. Sometimes we would eat at another base while we refueled the ship and rearmed the guns. One day, maybe it was August of '66, I was on a search-and-destroy mission. Tony was flying in the second ship and called me on the fox mic in our helmets to tell me to look down at the ground. As I did, the helicopter shook violently and I could see the ground exploding. *Holy Shit!* We were flying through a B52 bombing raid. I look up and all I see are things that look like bombs coming down. I switch on my mic so I can speak with the pilots, but how do I tell them? They were bright guys, so why not just say, "Hey guys, we are flying through a B52 raid; look down or look up, but let's get the flock out of here." I don't know how we got out of there so fast or how we did not get hit by one of the bombs. When we got back to base we all had a couple of drinks to calm down. The Robin Hoods crossbows spent two weeks in the Central

High Lands, which is home to a people called *montagnard*—a French word meaning mountain people. These people were living the same way they were 1,000 years before. So you can only image how they were treated by the Vietnamese. So they were friends of ours because their enemy was our enemy. We slept in our ships, ate nothing but C-rations. Tony, Ron, Tony's gunner, and I decide to play with the machine gun ammo. Every fifth round is a tracer round, meaning it leaves a red trail so you can see where you are hitting. So we load our M60 ammo with all tracers, so when we shot the 60, it looked like a flame thrower. However, we never thought of the consequences. It was late at night and so dark you couldn't see your hand. I'm on standby with Ron as my gunner. One of the montagnards gives us a bag we think is pot; this is the first time for me. As a crew chief, I was too high profile and always around the officers, so I couldn't be doing things I wasn't supposed to. I empty out a cigarette and fill it with the contents of the bag. I smoke it, but don't feel anything. I take another hit and then started to hallucinate. I was so messed up. It turns out the stuff in the bag was hashish. My ship was on standby and when my number 4-1-9 was called, Tony had to hide me, and he took my ship up with Ron. To this day, I wonder how I would have felt if something had happened to Tony that night.

The second week we were with the montagnards,

Ron unbeknownst to me, had smoked some of that same hashish and we wound up in the air in some real heavy shit. When I heard the pilot in the right seat yelling, "I'm hit, I'm getting hit! I'm getting hit in my feet and legs," I threw a can of red smoke out to mark the spot where the fire from the ground was coming from. I hoped the follow-up ship would come in behind us and shoot at the marked spot. The pilot is still yelling, so I look at Ron, and he is the one shooting the pilot! I call to him, "Ron! Stop!" But he didn't respond, so I reach over to his machine gun ammo cans and break the link to stop the ammo from feeding into the gun. Ron shot through the door and glass bubble and the skids, not to mention the pilot.

The next day, I got called in to tell the officers what happened: when the pilot pulled a 180 to the right, Ron was supposed to lean out to the right, but instead leaned into the ship. Ron went in after me and told them it wasn't his fault that we loaded our 60s with solid tracers and got target fixation. So Ron was in no trouble, the pilot was going home after his hospital stay in Japan, the Huey was getting fixed—all was as it should be. We were told, "Don't ever do that thing with the ammo again."

Finally out of the highlands, we came back to our base in Lai Khe and life went on as usual. We were still getting mortared because we had civilians from the village come in every day for work, like the laundry girls. We were fighting a war, so we had no time for this housekeeping stuff. But the civilians were making maps of the compound and giving them to the VC. Makes sense to me. This was war.

9

R&R

Weeks pass and it's time for R&R (rest and relaxation). The married guys went to Hawaii, otherwise you had to stay in the same part of the world as Vietnam, so Tony, Ron, and I chose Hong Kong. We couldn't wait! Our crew chief sergeant told Tony and me that two crew chiefs couldn't go on R&R at the same time, as the company can't be down two gunships for ten days. So, we Red X our ships. Now they need to be in the maintenance shop, and, of course, they won't be fixed in less than ten days since the guys in maintenance are so backed up.

"Go get the hell out of here, the three of you," the sergeant told us. So with the sergeants blessing we were off to Hong Kong. We got a ride on a Huey going to Saigon, slept overnight in the base, and by the next morning we were in clean khaki uniforms on the way to Hong Kong. Once there, we checked into The Presidente Hotel.

On our third day in Hong Kong, I placed a collect call to my oldest brother, Al, and asked him to wire me money. I never gave any thought to the time difference, which is twelve hours. He did get to say hello to my lady friend. To this day Al is still waiting for me to pay him back the money.

We were able to be just tourists, spending our first whole day there sightseeing. It was so nice not being shot at. We found a car dealer and I got to take a picture in a '63 Chevy convertible. I bought a shark's skin suit and wore it out that night to a place called the Blue Fox Bar, which was packed with all the Navy guys.

"We can't stay here," I said to the guys. "We're in civvies and there are only three of us; we will get killed."

We decided to leave and come back at midnight when the Navy guys will have to be back on ship. Sure enough, by twelve, the place was empty, and we could watch the go-go dancers all by ourselves. Whenever I hear the Los Bravos song "Black Is Black," I am taken back to that club. When I first left the States the go-go thing—the short skirts the dancing and the music—hadn't happened yet. It was the beginning of the British invasion and I was missing out on it back home.

So Ron goes over to one of the dancers, and he hits it off with her. She's British and has two friends, so they meet us at the *Star Ferry* at 3 pm the next day. The *Star Ferry* is the principle way to carry passengers across Victoria Harbor between Hong Kong Island and Kowloon. The girls—one British, one American, and one Chinese—lived and went to school on the Kowloon side. Ron was with the British girl; Tony hit it off with the American, and I went with the Chinese girl, who spoke English with a British accent. For the next five days we met them every day. They were our tour guides. Then Ron's girl had to go back to the club to work, and the American girl turned out to be the daughter of a diplomat at the U.S. embassy. When he found out what she was doing, he had a car track her down and pull her away from all of us, halting our adventure, just like that. Tony said we should leave it alone, because if we pissed off her father, we'd never get out of Vietnam.

To say it is tempting to go AWOL when you are on R&R is an understatement. We said goodbye to the girls, expressing our gratitude, and sharing with them how badly we didn't want to go back to war. They understood but reminded us that if we didn't go back, we'd go to jail. The American girl really liked Tony, so he gave her the address to where she could write to him. The American girl's father found out his daughter was still in touch with Tony and demanded she tell him the GI's name. When he read this in her letter, Tony flipped. "I'm never going home, man."

So I went to the mail clerk with the letter she wrote, took the stamper, and hit the envelope with RETURN TO SENDER KIA (Killed in Action).

10

Consequences

My ship was still in the maintenance shop, so I told Ron I'd fly with Tony and he could fly with Joe. He agree. Ron spoke with another gunner named Arthur who was a short-timer, meaning he had thirty days or less in country, and was on his way home. In the Crossbows, we had an unwritten policy that said when you hit thirty days, no more combat flying. Someone else would take your flights but when the ship came back you had to still do the daily inspection and maintenance (if you were a crew chief), rearm the ship, and clean the guns (if you were a gunner).

When Tony and I went back to our tent that night to get something to eat after we did our thing on the flight line, it was eerily quiet; you could hear a pin drop. *What's going on?*

In unison, five crew chiefs said, "You don't know?"

"Know what?"

"Ron is dead."

"What? Did a doughnut dolly kill him?" We couldn't figure out how else he could've died.

The crew chiefs looked at us like we had smoked too much hash.

"No, he went down with Joe's ship; everyone is dead."

Joe's dead?

"Ron isn't dead!" we answered. "He went across the runway to hang out with the doughnut dollies. He told us before we took off today. He asked Arthur to take his flight. Arthur said he was bored, so he said okay."

With that, we see Ron walking in, "Hi guys," he said without a care in the world. We all had to go to the operations tent to catch major hell.

"How can you change crew members without telling ops?" one officer screamed. "We were just about to send the letters out. Don't do that again, get out. NOW!"

That day Joe's ship was shot down and all on board were killed. It took Arthur two days to die of third degree burns. He was on his way home that month.

When I went to a reunion in Washington, D.C., in 2014, about twenty of us went to the wall at the Vietnam Memorial and found the names we knew. While a few guys were having the names of the dead stenciled on to paper, I couldn't do it. If I hadn't Red Xed my ship to go on R&R, this wouldn't have happened to Arthur. *Consequences.*

Later on that night in D.C., we were back at the hotel and having some drinks. I happened to mention to Gary and some other guys who were in our company how Arthur did not have to die; he wasn't supposed to be flying that day. Tony and I were passing a table where maybe fifteen guys were sitting. They invited us down for a drink. None of them knew the story about Arthur. Except for one.

"That was you guys," he said, "who caused the officer in flight operations to freak out?"

There was a long silence at the table.

11

Now Back to Our
Regularly Scheduled War

So a week or two passed by with just your everyday stuff going on: getting mortared at night, flying and shooting, and having company events designed to keep up moral. We had wheel barrel races, grease tree climbing—none of the things we kids from New York City did. *Where was the Johnny pump and stick ball? What? No Buick standing in for second base.*

One morning, as we were getting our orders for the day, I got the sense they wanted to separate Tony and me. I was to go on a search and destroy and Tony was on a search and destroy but in a different area. Ron told to me he was going back to hang with the doughnut dollies. I got very upset considering what happened with Artur. I told him, "I fly, you fly." I felt fate was the hunter. So we spent the day flying and landing at different bases, which I located on a map, to refuel. We were flying in what was called a free-fire area, because there were no friendlies around; just the enemy. When we refuel at Ben Cat, a Brigadier General came over to me and said, "Specialist, are you the crew chief?"

"Yes, sir, I am."

"Where is your AC air craft commander?"

I pointed him out, and the next thing I'm told is the General will be taking my seat. "Do you mind?" I'm asked, which was funny, because what if I did? So what? The General was rotating home and wanted to fly a gun ship one last time.

So with him now in charge, we're flying at 80 knots at 1,500 feet, and the General spoke into the fox mic, "Look at all the people on the ground. Let's go get them. What do you think, crew chief?"

He already had spoken to the second lieutenant on their radio channel. I knew the second lieutenant wouldn't go against a one-star General.

"The people are out in the open; we're not being shot at. It looks like they are waving," I answered.

"Let's drop down to 500 feet and then open up on them."

I switched my mic to Ron only. "There's no way I'm shooting unless we are shot at."

"Same for me."

Meanwhile the second ship had a call in to ops to question the designation of the area on the map. Turns out the area had been secured, and the family of the South Vietnam army was living there. No one shot. We just waved.

I still feel good about my decision.

12

Village Life

The villagers of Lai Khe were quite taken with the luxuries of America. In fact, many had never seen a Polaroid picture before. For a canned ham or a photo, soldiers were offered special "service." The *mama sans* would have their kids call out to us, "Haaaaay GI, my mamasan number one cherry girl; you want to meet her? It was ridiculous. How could her mama be a cherry girl? What people will do to survive. The villagers also called out to us, "Boo-coo Dinky Dow," which was a mix of French and Vietnamese, which translated into *very crazy in the head*.

Our close proximity with the villagers meant that venereal disease had become a big problem for the army, so it came up with this solution: build a big club with air conditioning, a bar, a dance floor, a stage for a band, and in the back put in as many rooms as possible. Then give the girls weekly physicals. If they are free of any form of VD, they get a tag to wear that indicates they are clean. If they have VD, they can't work, but they can hustle drinks at the bar. This actually worked wonders. The VD rate dropped. Now that we had a place to go, we could stop smuggling in the girls from the village across the runway.

Some of the days were made interesting just by the people we had in the company. Remember the mail clerk who helped me out with the KIA rubber stamp? He had a pet mongoose he used to run a gambling game. The guys in the infantry would catch a cobra and drop it in to a six-foot cage where the mongoose was. Who would you bet on?

Then one night the mail clerk was going on guard duty, which required him to be out all night, walking the perimeter of the base camp. It sucked. Thankfully, crew chief and gunners did not pull guard duty. The mail clerk was twirling his M14 around his trigger finger like a cowboy would a 6 gun and shot himself in the foot. As he left for the hospital in Saigon, his last words to me were, "Take care of the mongoose." When we found out a few days later the mail clerk would not be coming back to our company, we set the mongoose free, figuring he did his time in the Nam.

We had a dog we called Thing. Thing had the run of the company compound. He would go from tent to tent staying as long as he wanted and would move on to another tent. One day we came back from a mission by 5pm because the pilots liked to watch the show, "Batman," and that was the time the show aired on Armed Forces Television. But Thing wasn't there to greet us. We never saw him again. We figured one of the Vietnamese workers took him home and ate him.

Our company doctor was a neurosurgeon—no kidding, he was drafted. He would complain to anyone who would listen. "I can't believe I can cut open a brain and here I am doing short arm inspections," he'd say. He somehow acquired an organ and a monkey. He played the organ all night to annoy everyone, which worked. Even the company commander could not get him to stop. The monkey was the nastiest thing you would ever see. As you walked by the Doc's tent the monkey, which was on a twenty-foot rope, would try to get you. It spit at you, threw its dung at you, tried to bite you. One day the monkey got loose and went into another officer's tent and made a mess and escaped into the trees. When the officer came back to the tent, the Doc was out of camp. The officer took the opportunity to shoot the monkey out of the trees.

It had to be late August or early September and my ship had gotten a little beaten up, so it was in for maintenance. I was so bored that when I was asked to go on a convoy by truck to Saigon for supplies I said sure. While I was there I could go to the PX and buy some booze to bring back to the guys, who handed me their lists. I climbed into the back of the deuce-and-a-half truck with my M14 and settled in for a bumpy ride north on Highway 13. I was in one of the many trucks in the convoy. We picked up some cots and some foot lockers and wall lockers then headed to the PX. I bought a watch, a Zodiac, which I still have, and still works. That's when we found out we had to be twenty-one to buy liquor on a federal base. So that was the first of many things to go wrong.

Leaving the PX, I sat on top of all of the stuff we had just picked up, and the driver lost control of the truck, throwing me off. As I lay on the ground, the trailer that was hitched to the truck ran my leg over. I couldn't move, and was in excruciating pain. I saw the young face of a south Vietnamese soldier standing over me. He took my hand and said something to me. I don't know what it was, but it felt compassionate. *These are people too.*

In the ambulance, I couldn't move my legs. The doctor kept poking me in the small of my back, and I kept moving his hands away. "Hold him down," the doctor yelled.

I stayed in the hospital at Tan Son Nhat Air Base for ten days. For the first four days, I couldn't move; I was paralyzed from the waist down. The doctor told me it was because of the trauma to my back when I hit the ground. "Good thing you were wearing a flak jacket," said the doctor.

They wanted me to stay for two weeks but I was such a pain in the ass, calling my company every day and requesting a Huey to get me. Finally, the doctor gave up and signed me out. The Robin Hoods sent a CH47 Chinook for me. I was put on light duty for a week because my left leg was all bandaged up.

Tony became my caregiver. He changed my bandage, wrapped it in plastic so I could shower. When I was hungry, he went to the mess hall for me. Yes, he hated me at this point. I loved it. I never found out why the driver lost control. *Was he shot at? Did he hit a land mine or was he just a bad driver?*

Around this time, my two older brothers, Al and Monty, wrote to tell me of their plans to buy a piece of property on Ave X in Brooklyn and using it to garage their soda trucks and then maybe open a retail and wholesale beverage distributer. They want to know if I want in. *Do I want to go in? All I want is to get out.* I told them I couldn't give them an answer while in Vietnam.

13

Short-timer

Christmas Day, 1966

A year had passed since I received my draft notice. My mother and her sisters had probably started the fish for the beginning of the Eve feast, as we were twelve hours ahead of New York time. But, even though I couldn't be there, my year tour was almost half over. I was close to being a short-timer now.

The army said there was a cease fire in effect. I still heard the big 105 cannons going off all night. You can't get any sleep because they shake the ground; it's like being mortared. Christmas Day a small plane flew over the company area in very large circles like those little planes at the beach, except there was no advertisement being pulled behind it. Instead it was playing Christmas music. *Whose idea is this? Why doesn't someone shoot* him *down?* Tony told me to put my M14 away. Since then, I've never been known to love Christmas.

Knowing that each day brings you closer to being a short-timer you get to carry around a short stick so everyone knows, and every once in a while, for no other reason than because you can, you yell out, "SHORT!" Followed by how many days left you have in country. This sounds like fun except there was always someone shorter, so they'd yell back, "SHORTER!"

The days went by with us doing the same thing most of the time: get up, go out for roll call to see who made it through the night, eat, work, fight, play, sleep, and do it again the next day. Except for this one day when I was hanging around waiting for the guys to come home, a pilot says, "I need to go to Tan Son Nhat, and I need a crew chief; you can fly left seat." Throwing caution to the wind, I said okay. I knew I was going home, so he told me to take the stick. "Go fly; it's fun."

So I flew the ship myself to Tan Son Nhat. I asked him if I could land. "Don't press your luck," was his reply. I stayed with the ship, while the pilot went out for about an hour.

Because I was sitting in the left seat, guys were walking passed me and saluting me because they thought I was a pilot. Out of the corner of my eye I see a few South Vietnamese ARVN(Army of the Republic of Vietnam) solders coming toward the ship, and they have guns. I jumped out of the front left seat and went in the back took my M60, locked and loaded it, and pointed it at the ARVNs. I still did not trust them. Seeing me pointing the 60 at them, made them change their direction.

I thought if I had to shoot or if I had made a mistake and shot, that would not have been the way to end my tour. When they were gone I went back up front and thought this who day called for a souvenir—so I took the eight-day clock, which is over my shadowbox in my office. The pilot got back and said suspiciously, "Something is missing, what's missing?"

"I don't know what you're talking about."

Never volunteer.

So now I am a short-timer with thirty days or less left in country and I heard the news on Arm Forces Radio about the demonstrations back home, and that the men who serve in Vietnam are called baby killers. I know it's not a popular war, thanks to my two older brothers writing me to tell me they would get into heated arguments with people who would refer to me like that. We were so isolated from all of it, so far removed, which is ironic to me now, so hearing it and then coming home to it was nothing less than a shock. I could not prepare myself for things to come.

At this point, Tony and Ron and I are beginning to have separation anxiety. We told each other that we would see each other again but Ron didn't believe it since he was all the way in California and actually thought I would forget him. That is funny now, since we talk all the time, going on fifty years later.

Because we live in the same city, Tony asked me to

go visit his parents for him, and I promised I would, and I did have macaroni with them with my cousin Caesar at their house off Gunhill Road.

We got mortared one more time before I left. *Why not?* Tony went for his ship and Ron went for his ship, and I was not flying because I was a short-timer, so I headed for the bunker.

"Man, what are you, nuts?" Tony said. "We built those things."

While both of us are trying to make up our minds about where I should go, guys are yelling around us as the mortars come in, "Make up your effin' minds! You are going to die!" Tony went up, and I stayed in the bunker. We both got lucky that night.

My last helicopter ride was not as thrilling as my first one, almost 365 days earlier. I was in my tent saying my goodbyes, and I saw the Huey that was going to take me to Tan Son Nhat, so that's it ... got to go. I go outside the tent and as I was heading for the Huey, the CO comes over to me to say goodbye. What he said next, I never saw coming. "You have done a fine job, and I am proud to have had you in my command." And all I can think is *what if the Huey takes off without me?*

I got in and for as long as I could see the company area, I keep looking back at it. It seems I am still looking back.

14

Going Home

It was only a twenty-minute flight to Tan Son Nhat, where I waited in my jungle fatigues to board the jumbo jet heading to San Francisco with stops in Guam and Hawaii. The plane was full of soldiers going home to the real world. As the jet wheels left the ground, in unison we let out a loud cheer. A little while later the pilot's voice came over the loud speaker.

"We are out of Vietnamese air space."

Hooray!!

Then again from the cockpit, "The bar is now open."

Hooray! Hooraaaay!

We landed first in Oakland and got off the plane and tried to wrap my head about how just a few hours ago I was in the jungle. It dawned on me, *I made it*. We were to be fitted for our summer dress uniforms while in California, and within one hour I'm finished, so I hope in a cab and leave the base.

The cabbie says, "Where to?"

"The city by the bay."

My plane left for New York City the next day. I left alone and came home alone, not like the guys in World War II who went together and came home together and had thirty days at sea to make the huge adjustment. In less the twenty-four hours I was back in the real world, and I no longer recognized it.

As the jet taxied to the gate I looked out the window and saw my mother and father and two younger brothers Robert and Michael. I got so nervous, I thought I was going to become sick. I was eager to show my parents and family how I looked in my uniform, but people were not looking at me nicely. In fact, I was picking up some real hostile vibes. *I was safer in Vietnam; at least I had a gun. What did I come home to?* I knew I had to get out of my uniform fast.

"Let's leave now," I say to my parents nervously. I wouldn't know until decades later that that nervousness was one of the first symptoms of my post-traumatic stress disorder (PTSD).

My father let me drive home; he must have *really* missed me. As I pulled up to our house on Dahill Road, I saw a metal sign:

WELCOME HOME DANNY
FROM VIETNAM

Most of my cousins and aunts and uncles were there, my other brothers and all the neighbors, and I lost my mind, just freaked out. I jumped out of the car, ripped the sign from the house, threw it on the ground, and passed by everyone and went inside the house. My father died without ever asking me about that day. After his death I thought about how I should've probably apologized.

I had thirty days on leave before I had to finish my tour of six more months of duty in Ft. Rucker, Alabama. While home, I worked on the trucks. My father wouldn't have tolerated me hanging around, doing nothing, for a month. One morning my mother came into my room and placed her hands on me and shook me to wake me up. I jumped up and started to choke her. She never did that again. My brother Monty on the other hand thought it was funny, and every chance he had he would wake me knowing he would be tougher to choke. He did this until I learned to ignore him.

A few days before leaving for Alabama, I got really sick. Our family doctor, Dr. Kanner, happened to be a lieutenant colonel in the army reserves. He gave me a prescription for an antibiotic and a note to give headquarters when I reported to Ft. Rucker. The sergeant took my orders and gave them to the lieutenant who gave them to the captain. I was told to go to report to the doctor, and he admitted me to the infirmary. What a way to start my last six months of active duty. Tony also had orders to report to Ft. Rucker. *This may not be so bad after all.* When he found out I was in the hospital, he somehow got himself admitted to the bed next to me, just like old times.

I was an instructor teaching a class of wannabe crew chiefs. *Are you kidding?* The only thing they learned from me is how to have a bad attitude. I did have a bad attitude, but not with the new recruits; I was constantly locking horns with my sergeant, an E5. He was a state-side guy, who hadn't been to Nam so everything to him was by the book. *Come on. A month ago I was living in a tent getting shot at being mortared, shitting in a 55-gallon drum, which I had to burn with diesel fuel. I was told not to salute any officers on the flight line for fear of them being shot by a sniper, and now you want me to tuck in my shirt, shine my boots, say "yes sir," "no sir," and listen to your bull?!*

I didn't only think all of that, I *said* it to him. I finally told him to get out of my face, after which he reported me to the top—an E7 who was in the Nam. "If you didn't have such a bad attitude, you could make E5," he told me.

"You can make me a civilian," was my answer.

"What is wrong with you?" he asked me. It was a rhetorical question.

I was drafted; that's what wrong with me.

He asks, again, rhetorically, "Why can't you go along to get along?"

I did go along. All this means nothing. It don't mean a thing.

Here is where I crossed the line.

"The army should not have sent me here," I told him. "I should've been discharged after Nam. I can't, and I don't want to play solider. You think you are special because you went to Nam? No. I'm not a lifer, like you. Go eff yourself."

I was reported to the lieutenant who was new and had not yet been deployed. He told me what a disgrace I was to the uniform. It would take me forty years to know he was wrong, that I did my part, and I'm proud of my service.

In response, I reminded him that the life expectancy of a second lieutenant in a hot LZ in Nam was sixteen minutes. That didn't go over well. He told me he was going to make me guard Dr. Pepper vending machines from midnight to dawn on top of my daytime work until I was discharged from active duty. I pulled my first night of guard duty, and in the morning, instead of hitting the sack, I waited for headquarters to open and went to see the lieutenant colonel, who happened to be the CO in Nam, who said goodbye to me as I boarded the Huey to go home.

"Ok, so why now what did you do?" he asked me.

I told him all of it.

"You are straight up absolutely wrong. You should be thrown in jail," he said. "But, no one I flew with in combat and who had my back is going to guard vending machines over this bullshit."

So for the next few months I was bullet proof and some of the armor rubbed off on Tony. We had a blast spending every weekend in Panama City.

Time went by. Nothing unusual, just every day getting me one day closer to getting out. But you never really get out.

Afterword

It took some time for the American people to wake up and realize this was a bull shit war, but when they did, it got ugly. The protesting started slowly at the college and university levels. By the time I was discharged from the army, the protesting was in full force. Although I was against the war, I took no active part in any protest. How could I not be against a war that went on so long that my younger brother Michael's draft number came up. He is nine years younger than me. *Are you kidding me!* Looking back, I have a personal favorite protest slogan: *Hey! Hey! LBJ! How many kids did you kill today?* Today, I now know it was Eisenhower who actually started the whole damn thing.

The slogan is only my favorite now because it called out the president who was responsible for putting me in Vietnam. Just for the record it still bothers me that some people called us baby killers.

Years later, after the PTSD diagnosis and the cancer I got, thanks to Agent Orange exposure, I requested a Purple Heart for when I was thrown off the truck and run over by the trailer, but because I had no medical records of the incident, the request was denied. I requested my records from the army, and was told if they did exist, they likely had been destroyed during the Tet Offensive during Christmas 1969. I even went to my local congressman, and he did a congressional search, but nothing came up. The letter of denial read in part, "This should not diminish your proud service to our country. Thank you and goodbye."

I had previously tried to file a claim with the VA because I was having trouble with my left knee and lower back, but I was turned away because my medical records were lost in the Tet Offensive. But there was another reason: At the time, the VA was being run by the guys from WW2. Their attitude was that America never lost a war, but here come the Baby Boomers who did, because in their opinion we were more interested in smoking dope than winning a war. So they made things difficult for all the Vietnam vets.

A few years ago, with the help of my PTSD support group leader, Tom McGoldrick, Ph.D. who, by the way, gave me the help I needed to write about Vietnam in the first place, I filed again because of cancer and a heart attack that led to four stents. I could be and should be angry with the VA after they admitted it was the army's fault for my heart attack and cancer and PTSD. Someone in the government had to know the long-term effects of Agent Orange, or should have, as it is now linked to at least a dozen other diseases, some of which can be passed on to the vets' children.

The VA finally began sending me monthly benefits, which came in handy because I was no longer working. But after five years, I received a letter stating that my cancer payments would stop because I was no longer in treatment. Once you are "cured," you are cut off. I went to my cancer doctor, and asked him if I was cured and he said, "You are never cured; you are in remission." I opened up my case to appeal and went through all the crap again. When I went to see the shrink at the VA in Manhattan, he agreed to advocate for me.

After waiting eighteen months, the VA increased my PTSD diagnosis. It seems I had it all along but dealt with it by drinking and working. This did not come to the surface until I had to stop working and seek out counseling.

Am I sorry I went to Vietnam? Would I do the same thing over again? I made some good friends over there and maybe the experience helped shape who I would be in later life. All I really know is, it don't mean a thing.

57104632R00048

Made in the USA
Lexington, KY
06 November 2016